Swimming Coloring Book

FOR KIDS 4-8

inkHORSE Publishing

This Book Belongs to:

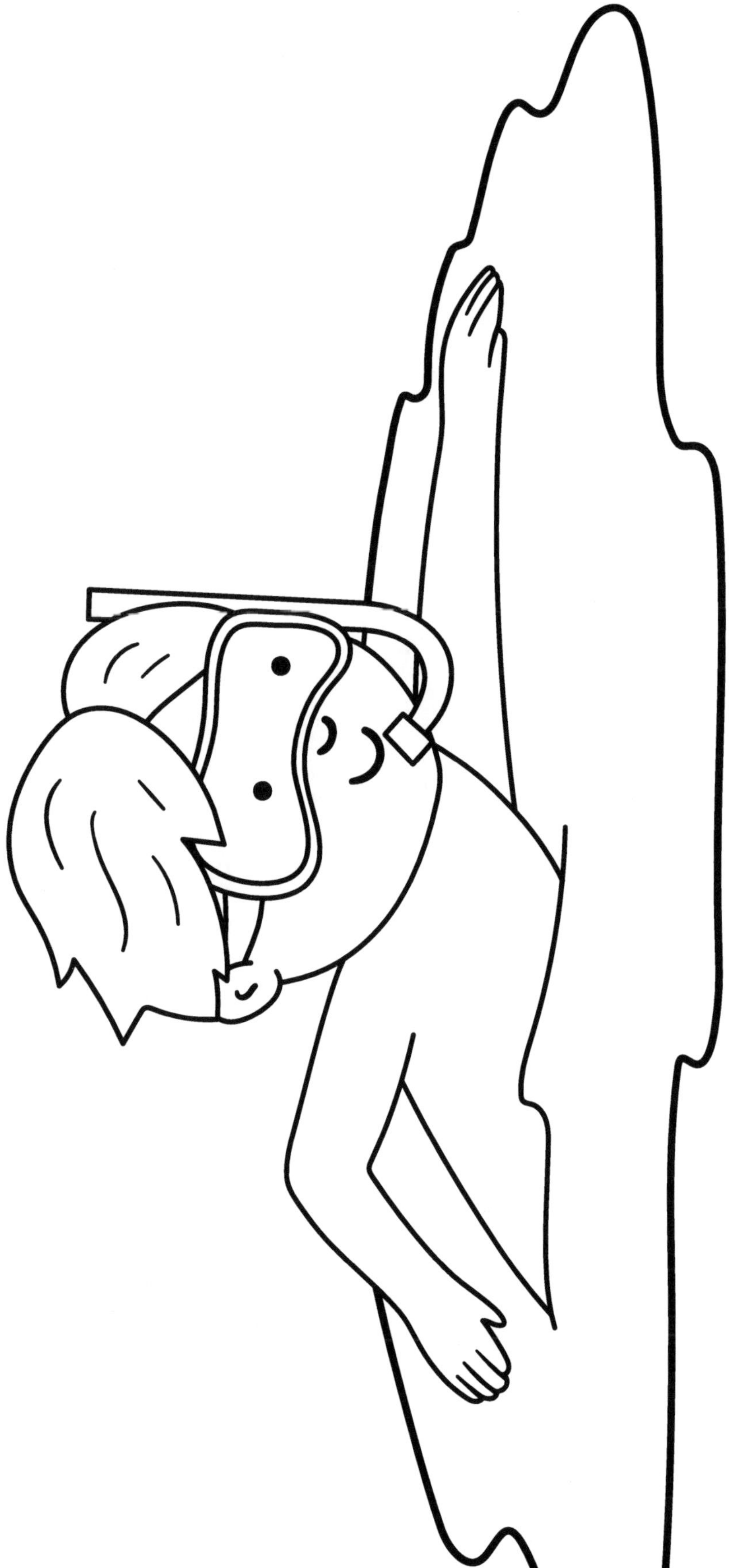

Ice-cream

SUN
SCREEN

SUN
SCREEN

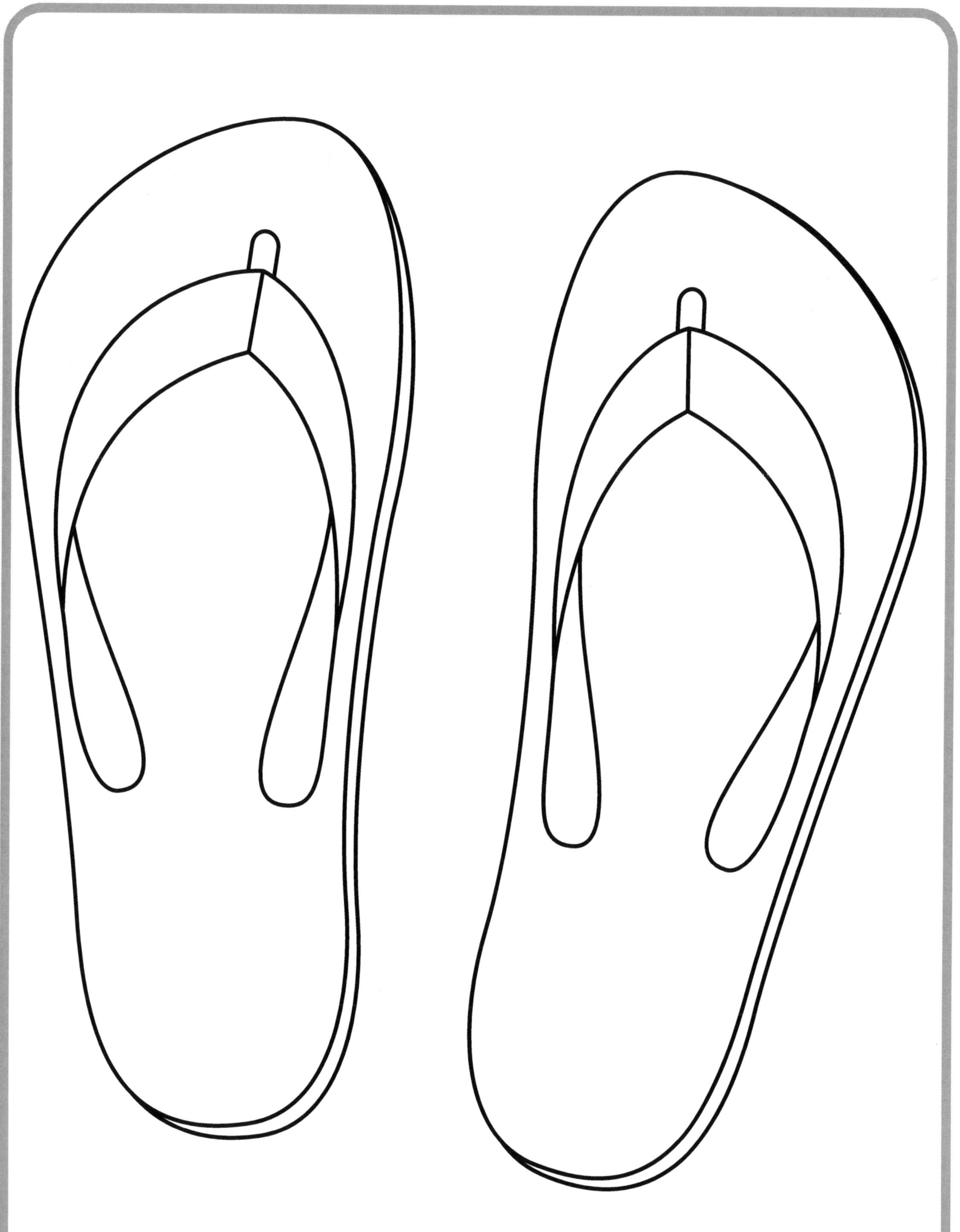

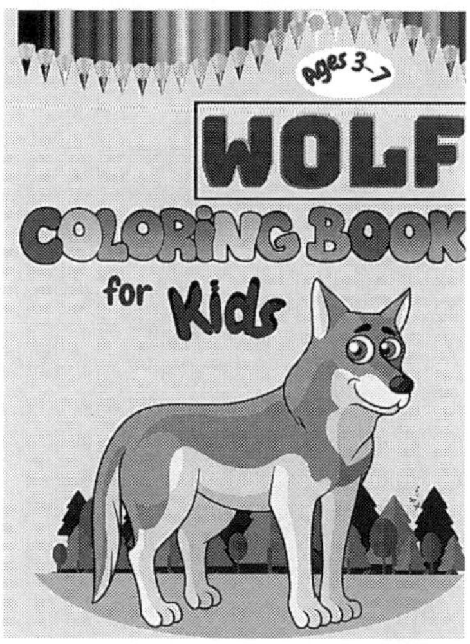

FOR MORE BOOKS SCAN THE QR CODE

Thank you!

inkHORSE Publishing

Made in United States
Orlando, FL
11 September 2024

51383042R00057